GROWING TOGETHER IN

FORGIVENESS

GROWING TOGETHER IN

FORGIVENESS

READ-ALOUD STORIES FOR **FAMILIES**

FAMILYLIFE®

Little Rock, Arkansas

BARBARA RAINEY

GROWING TOGETHER IN FORGIVENESS

FamilyLife Publishing®
5800 Ranch Drive
Little Rock, Arkansas 72223
1-800-FL-TODAY • FamilyLife.com
FLTI, d/b/a FamilyLife®, is a ministry of Campus Crusade for Christ International®

Unless otherwise noted, Scripture quotations are taken from the New American Standard Bible®, Copyright © 1960, 1962, 1963, 1968, 1971, 1972, 1973, 1975, 1977, 1995 by The Lockman Foundation. Used by permission. (www.Lockman.org)

ISBN: 978-1-60200-524-2

Design: Brand Navigation, LLC
Photograph of Te Rongopai a Ruka (The Gospel of Luke in Māori) by Bruce Hutton QSM, FPSNZ. © Bible Society New Zealand. Used with permission.

Printed in the United States of America
2012—First Edition

16 15 14 13 12   1 2 3 4 5

FAMILYLIFE®
Help for today. Hope for tomorrow.

dedicated to

Savannah Rainey—

There is nothing more beautiful
than a heart that loves by
freely forgiving.
May you become known
as a gracious woman who forgives,
for then you will be
more like Jesus.
He is the One who forgives infinitely.
He is the One who has forgiven you.
And He is the One who will show you the way
all the days of your life.

CONTENTS

WHY FORGIVENESS

I know a family in which two brothers haven't spoken in years and another family in which a brother and sister haven't spoken in decades. Sadly, this is firsthand knowledge for me; all four individuals are in my extended family. There are no perfect family trees, because there are no perfect people.

Something happened within both sets of siblings: a perceived offense, a genuine hurt, a jealousy; all unresolved. And now everyone walks on eggshells. Not speaking at all or pretending all is well when it is not are the same thing. Both are evidence of hearts with walls built around them.

Often overlooked is how this affects others: children, friends, family, and most importantly, God. Our Father in Heaven grieves. He and the parents on earth cry for the joy and beauty that has been lost, destroyed by a lack of forgiveness.

Henri Nouwen wrote, "Forgiveness is love practiced among people who love poorly." In our poor loving, we hurt others intentionally and unintentionally—and are hurt ourselves. He adds, "It is freeing to become aware that we do not have to be victims of our past and can learn new ways of responding. But there is a step beyond this recognition . . . it is the step of forgiveness."[1]

Because we love poorly we must forgive frequently. It is not a "one and done" action, as we might wish. Repetition is necessary. Humility is also needed, for we must bow before God Himself. It is He who instructs us to forgive. He is the One to whom we must answer. He alone is the Judge who knows all hearts.

MATTERS

And ultimately, the power of forgiveness lies in its ability to replay God's forgiveness over and over in our lives. Even among non-Christians, forgiveness proclaims the need for restoration to our Maker and to one another. Forgiveness announces the gospel and its unparalleled healing power to a broken world.

Forgiveness may not take away the pain or be well received. But without it the hurt will only grow deeper, hardening us. We have an amazing capacity for denial, for pretending, and for masking. But the One who sees all knows when we are trying to protect, guard, and keep up appearances. C. S. Lewis said, "To love at all is to be vulnerable. . . . The only place outside Heaven where you can be perfectly safe from all the dangers and perturbations of love is Hell."[2]

Reading dozens of stories to find these seven, I've been amazed at the transformative power of forgiveness. My prayer is that these men, women, and children will inspire you to say, *If they believed God's power was sufficient, if they could forgive, then I can, too.* May your family become strong, courageous forgivers!

Barbara Rainey

November 2011

FORGIVENESS

MEMORY VERSE

"As for you, you meant evil against me,
but God meant it for good."
—GENESIS 50:20

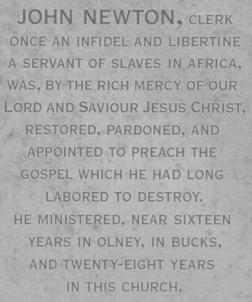

JOHN NEWTON, CLERK
ONCE AN INFIDEL AND LIBERTINE
A SERVANT OF SLAVES IN AFRICA,
WAS, BY THE RICH MERCY OF OUR
LORD AND SAVIOUR JESUS CHRIST,
RESTORED, PARDONED, AND
APPOINTED TO PREACH THE
GOSPEL WHICH HE HAD LONG
LABORED TO DESTROY.
HE MINISTERED, NEAR SIXTEEN
YEARS IN OLNEY, IN BUCKS,
AND TWENTY-EIGHT YEARS
IN THIS CHURCH.

unchained
forgiveness is a gift received

One of the most famous songs ever written came from a very unlikely pen. Though the words were written over 230 years ago, this tune is still sung today around the world. See if you can guess the name of the song before the end of this story.

In 1725, a ship captain's wife gave birth to a baby boy whom they named John. When John turned eleven, he joined his father at sea, becoming the ship's cabin boy. If you've seen any pirate movies you've had a glimpse of what sailors were often like, unclean and uncivilized. Months and even years at sea hardened these men on the outside and on the inside. A ship was not an ideal environment for young John.

When he was a teenager, a gang of sailors from another ship kidnapped John and carried him away to serve on their ship. He tried to escape, but was caught and beaten for trying to run. The captain hated him, and the sailors taunted him. The ship was like a prison. John wrote in his journal that his heart was "filled . . . with bitter rage, and black despair."[1]

> If we confess our sins, He is faithful and righteous to forgive us our sins and to cleanse us from all unrighteousness.
> —1 JOHN 1:9

> He tried to escape, but was caught and beaten for trying to run.

Eventually the captain abandoned John, leaving him to work for a British slave trader on the African coast. While there, John became gravely ill and almost died. His hard life had gotten worse, and then worse again. He felt hopeless, alone, and forsaken.

But God saw John. He had not forgotten him. God was working a good plan for John's life.

After recovering from his illness, John was taken by another slave trader on a ship bound for England. Thoughts of home renewed his hope. He remembered his father and mother and Mary, the young woman he had fallen in love with before being kidnapped. But when the ship sailed southwest to Brazil, his despair returned. John became the worst of the sailors: cursing his shipmates, cursing God, and drinking hard liquor until he passed out.

In the providence of God, John found a book on the ship called *The Imitation of Christ*. As he read it, he realized that he was lost and wasting his life. Remembering the truth he had learned as a child and the many times God had saved his life made John want to be whole and clean again.

He concluded that there had never been such a sinner as he, and he wondered if his sins were too awful to be forgiven.

Months later the ship docked, and John immediately went to a church to pray. There, he surrendered his heart and life to the will of God. He received forgiveness from the One he had most offended.

John was free from the prison of the ship and more importantly free from the wicked life he had lived all those years at sea. Upon returning to England he asked Mary to be his wife, promising he would provide for her and live a godly life. She agreed. But the only way John knew how to earn a living was at sea, so back to the ocean he went, this time as the captain of a slave ship. As a new Christian, John had yet to understand the evil of the slave trade, but he did vow to treat the slaves well, unlike other captains who treated them as animals.

Even at the rank of captain, John found his vocation difficult. Think of it like this: If it's raining outside, and you don't want to get wet, even though an umbrella or raincoat can help, the best way to stay dry is to stay inside. For John, returning to life at sea was like going outside in a rainstorm. Even though he tried to "cover up" by reading his Bible and praying every morning, he found that being in the company of the wicked sailors and earning his living through the slave trade, made it nearly impossible to live the godly life he desired. John gave himself to God anew, writing, "Not by my own power and holiness, but by the mighty power and promise of God, through faith in an unchangeable Saviour."[2]

Believing it was time to retire from sailing, John became a pastor. He befriended William Wilberforce who was working diligently to bring an end to the slave trade in England. As one who had made his living carrying slaves in his ship, John's voice was a powerful one against the evils of slavery.

Have you thought of the song John wrote? He wrote a collection of hymns, the most famous of which is "Amazing Grace." He once wrote to a friend, "So much forgiveness, so little love . . . Such great privileges, and a life so sadly below them."[3] John Newton never forgot what he had been and how great the forgiveness he had received by the grace of God.

questions about forgiveness

Learning to forgive others begins with being forgiven by God first, because all our sin and all our rebellion is against Him. Be sure, today, that you have received God's forgiveness.

- John Newton felt that his life had gone from bad to worse. Have you ever felt that way? What did you do to try to make things better?
- How should you pray in times like that?
- Have you confessed your sin to God and received His forgiveness through Christ's sacrifice?

practicing forgiveness

God is willing to forgive us on the basis of His love and the sacrifice of His son Jesus. You can't do anything to earn God's forgiveness; He offers it as a gift. When people do wrong to you, don't retaliate. Be like Jesus and forgive them.

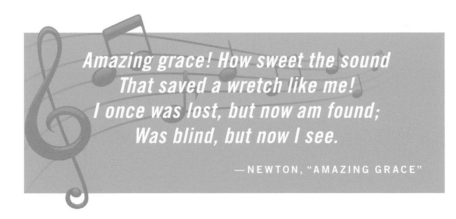

Amazing grace! How sweet the sound
That saved a wretch like me!
I once was lost, but now am found;
Was blind, but now I see.

—NEWTON, "AMAZING GRACE"

praying together for forgiveness

Thank you, Jesus, that You did not become discouraged in what the Father gave You to do on Earth. You did not quit when it was painful, but You accomplished Your work. You willingly forgave the thief hanging next to You. You willingly and eagerly forgive us when we ask. Thank You, Jesus, for carrying my sins on the cross, for dying for me, so that I, like the thief, might know the amazing grace of forgiveness. Amen.

Learn more about Negro Spirituals and "Amazing Grace" by viewing Wintley Phipps, *God Bless America*, DVD, Gaither Gospel Series (Alexandria, IN: Spring House Productions, 2002).

dreams come true

forgiveness is a gift given

Have you ever felt that life isn't fair? Maybe it seems to you that someone else, a brother or sister or a friend at school, gets more attention than you. Perhaps the kids down the street have lots of nice toys, new clothes, and their own cell phones, but they're not grateful for what they have and they're selfish. Maybe a friend has turned against you, and you don't know why.

You know what unfair feels like, don't you? It can make you angry and sad.

The problem is God *wants* us to be angry at injustice. He wants us to stand up for those who are being bullied and mistreated. But we must be careful when we feel that we have personally been treated unfairly. Our emotions can take over and cause us to do some very foolish things. That's what happened in one of the Bible's most unforgettable stories.

Joseph's father Jacob was very wealthy and owned many sheep. Joseph and his ten older brothers were shepherds. Joseph was his dad's favorite, and the brothers knew it. When young Joseph came home one day and tattled on his older brothers, they became angry. Then Joseph

> As for you, you meant evil against me,
> *but* God meant it for good.
>
> —GENESIS 50:20

His father was disturbed this time, and the brothers began to hate Joseph.

told them about a dream he had in which his brothers all bowed down to him. Instead of being interested in the dream, they were jealous. Then he had another dream that was similar to the first. Joseph could have kept these dreams to himself, but he was so excited that he told his family again. Even his father was disturbed this time, and the brothers began to hate Joseph.

Hating another person can lead to all kinds of evil. Like a volcano that simmers and rumbles before it finally erupts, Joseph's brothers spent hours and hours plotting how to solve their baby brother problem.

One day, when Jacob sent Joseph to check on his brothers, the volcano of their anger finally erupted. "Let us kill him," they said. But the oldest brother overruled and rescued Joseph from their hands. Plan B was then to throw Joseph into a pit, which led to Plan C: sell Joseph as a slave to an approaching caravan, which they did. After the caravan disappeared over the horizon, the brothers created a story—a lie—to tell their father. They told him that Joseph had been killed by a wild animal.

In Egypt, where Joseph was taken, he was sold again to an officer in the army. Later he was unfairly sent to prison for something he did not do. Life was not going well for Joseph. But instead of being angry, Joseph believed God was with him. He believed God was to be trusted, feared, and obeyed. So he waited for God to work.

Years later, he was released from prison when Pharaoh heard that he had the ability to interpret dreams. Because of Joseph's wisdom, which came from God, he was named second-in-command over the whole land of Egypt.

Fast forward the story about twelve years and Joseph was busy meeting with people from all over the world who had come to request food in order to survive a severe famine.* Joseph controlled the food supply. And who showed up begging for food? His brothers. But they didn't recognize him after so many years.

Joseph devised a plan, not to get even or to seek revenge, but to see his father. He told his brothers that they must come back later with the rest of the family if they wanted more food. When they returned, Joseph revealed who he was. They were so overcome with guilt that they bowed before him—just as he had dreamed they would when he was a boy.

Joseph's family had a severe case of sibling rivalry. Many times brothers and sisters find it difficult to love one another as God intended, but Joseph showed us how one person can change a family. As a ruler in Egypt, he could have ordered his ten older brothers killed for what they had done to him. Instead he chose God's way, saying to his brothers, "Do not be afraid," and they had reason to fear what Joseph could do to them. Then Joseph added, "You meant evil against me, but God meant it for good."

Forgiveness means not punishing the person who hurts you, but letting God do the disciplining. God sees everything that happens, and He will make all things right. The Bible says, "Never take your own revenge . . . 'I will repay,' " says the Lord" (Romans 12:19).

---

* See Reference Points on page 33.

questions about forgiveness

- In what ways is forgiving someone like giving them a gift?
- Why is it important that we learn to forgive others, especially our siblings?
- Why do you think it is oftentimes so hard to forgive?
- Joseph said to his brothers, "You meant evil against me, but God meant it for good." Why didn't Joseph take revenge on them?

practicing forgiveness

Sometimes people may hurt you again and again, and the hurt can last a long time. But there's something you can do to help the pain go away—you can forgive. Joseph became a better man and leader because he refused to hold a grudge against his brothers. Are you holding any grudges?

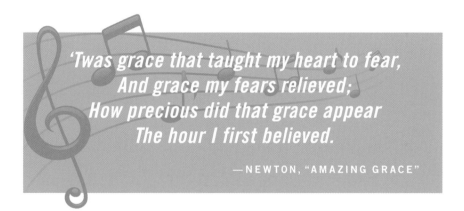

'Twas grace that taught my heart to fear,
And grace my fears relieved;
How precious did that grace appear
The hour I first believed.

—NEWTON, "AMAZING GRACE"

praying together for forgiveness

Our example of forgiveness is You, dear Jesus. You have called us to be like You. Help us follow Your words to Peter when he asked how many times he must forgive his brother and You replied, "Not seven times, but seventy times seven." May we give the gift of forgiveness over and over as You do for us. Amen.

You can read the story of Joseph in your Bible in Genesis chapters 37–50.

just one child

forgiveness is a gift of sacrifice

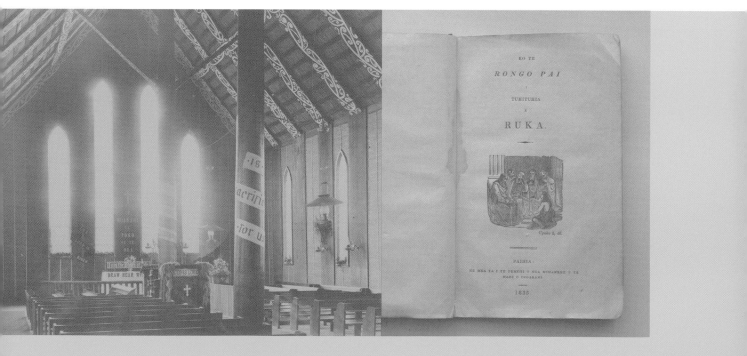

Have you ever watched toddlers playing together? Little children are not afraid to express how they feel when one of them knocks down the block tower they've just built together. The other child may throw a block or hit his playmate or run to tattle. It's called revenge. Adults also seek revenge and often cause great harm in the process.

The island country of New Zealand* was uninhabited for many centuries because of its remote location in the South Pacific. In the eleventh or twelfth century, islanders from Polynesia found the land and settled there. These new inhabitants, called Maori (mou´-ree), developed a system of rules for living not unlike the rules children often live by: the laws of revenge.

In the early 1800s, British explorers also discovered the island and began settlements. They were soon followed by missionaries who left homes, friends, and all that was familiar because they were passionate about sharing the love of Christ with those who did not know Him. The Bible teaches that without faith in Christ we are lost on Earth and lost from Heaven. At great cost,

If You, LORD, should mark iniquities,
O Lord, who could stand?
But there is forgiveness with You.

—PSALM 130:3—4

These new inhabitants developed a system of rules for living: the laws of revenge.

missionaries went to all the world to do the work of rescuing people from slavery to man's ways to the freedom of God's ways. Years of work were necessary to learn the local languages, develop a system of writing, and then to translate the Bible into the native people's language.

Alfred and Charlotte Brown arrived as missionaries to New Zealand in 1835. Soon they began a mission school to teach the Maori children to read and write in their own language. One of the first students was Tarore (tah´-rah-reh), the daughter of Ngakuku (nah´-ku-kuh), a relative of a famous chief. She was a very bright student who quickly learned to read.

Her missionary friends gave her a copy of the gospel of Luke as a gift. Tarore treasured her book and carried it safely around her neck in a straw purse. When she returned to her tribe every evening from school, she read the stories of Jesus to anyone who would listen. With fatherly pride,

---

* See Reference Points on page 33.

11

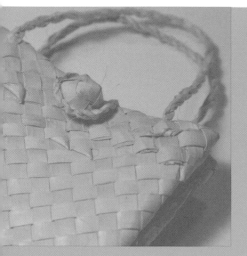

Ngakuku listened to his little girl reading and soon he believed that Jesus' way to live was better than the rules of his tribe. He gave his life to Christ to follow His way forever.

But times were troubled in the land of the Maori. Fighting was an ongoing way of life among the tribes. The Browns realized they needed to move the mission school to a safer location, and some Maori children were allowed to go with them to continue their schooling. Led by Tarore's father, the missionaries and the children caravanned to the new location, camping along the way at night. One evening, their cooking fires attracted the attention of a neighboring tribe. Later, when all were sleeping, the warriors crept toward them intending to kill the entire group. But when a dog barked out a warning, everyone fled into the forest. All except twelve-year-old Tarore, who had not heard and did not wake up. She alone was killed by the warriors. One of them found her little book, the gospel of Luke, in the purse she always carried, and though he had no idea what it was, he took it.

When Ngakuku found her body, he was overwhelmed with grief. Yet in his sadness he remembered the words Tarore read from Jesus: "Love your enemies" (Matthew 5:44) and "Forgive and you will be forgiven" (see Matthew 6:14). Before he found Jesus he would have demanded *utu*,* the payment of a life for a life. Now Ngakuku knew revenge was not the way. He sacrificed his feelings of revenge, of wanting to punish the man who killed his daughter, for the higher call to love his enemies.

The warrior who stole the little book was curious about its contents, so he found someone who taught him what it said. As he listened, he too believed the words of Jesus and felt great regret that he had killed Tarore. He decided to ask for forgiveness. Walking a great distance and taking a great risk that he might be killed in revenge, this warrior found both Tarore's father and forgiveness. Their story, along with other copies of the Bible, spread among the tribes leading many to choose the way of peace that Jesus taught. Even the greatest of their chiefs became a Christian and built a church for his people.

Today, in New Zealand, descendants of both the Maori tribes and the white settlers learn the story of Tarore in school. They learn that it was missionaries who brought Christianity to the native people, but it was the people themselves who shared the way of forgiveness with one another.

---

* See Reference Points on page 33.

questions about forgiveness

- What does "sacrifice" mean?
- In what way was it a sacrifice for Ngakuku to not take revenge?
- Why do you think the story of Tarore has made such an impression on the people of New Zealand for so many years?
- Will you decide to be like Ngakuku and be known for giving the gift of forgiveness to any who offend or hurt you?

practicing forgiveness

You don't have to be all grown up to make a difference and to set a good example. Remember that Tarore's father learned to love his enemies because of what she had read to him from the Bible. Start reading your Bible regularly now, and learn to live by its teachings while you're young.

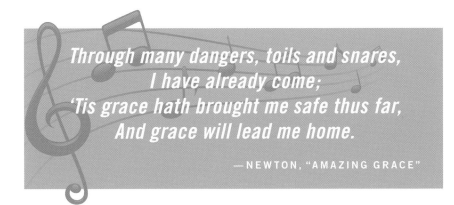

*Through many dangers, toils and snares,
I have already come;
'Tis grace hath brought me safe thus far,
And grace will lead me home.*

—NEWTON, "AMAZING GRACE"

praying together for forgiveness

Your Word tells us to turn away from evil and do good, to seek peace and pursue it. Help us be willing to sacrifice our desire for revenge so that we can choose to give the gift of forgiveness. May we remember that we become more like Jesus when we forgive. More like Jesus—may this be our greatest desire. Amen.

prankster and prisoner

forgiveness is a gift of freedom

There is an English word that has been used to describe many boys—mischievous, which means to play tricks or pranks, to annoy, or even to cause damage or injury. *Mischievous* perfectly described Louie Zamperini.

On his first escapade, Louie climbed out his bedroom window when he was just two years old, because he didn't want to stay inside. Pneumonia wasn't going to keep him in bed! As he grew older, his mischief became more daring. One of his favorite pranks was to steal food from neighbors' kitchens, the local bakery, country farms, and from homes in town where parties were being hosted. He didn't steal because he was hungry but because he liked the challenge of picking locks and seeing what he could get away with. Spankings from his parents did nothing to discourage him; Louie seemed untamable.

Louie sometimes recruited helpers, and for his crowning achievement Louie chose his older brother, Pete, to assist him. Louie climbed the steeple of the local Baptist church, tied a wire to

Let the wicked forsake his way
And the unrighteous man his thoughts;
And let him return to the Lord.
—ISAIAH 55:7

For forty-seven days these two men fought sharks . . . fished for something to eat, and held on for dear life.

its bell, and then strung the wire to a nearby tree. When the work was complete, the two boys hid high in the tree and started ringing the bell. Amazed, many of the townspeople thought it was a sign from God.

By the time he entered his teens, Louie had grown hard and angry, but his rescue was near. Pete was determined to save his little brother from self-destruction. Pete knew that one reason Louie was rarely caught was because he could run fast, so Pete began a campaign to channel Louie's energy in a positive direction. Forcing Louie to practice track every day, Pete encouraged Louie's hidden talent. Within a year he was winning races, loving the applause of the fans, and dreaming of breaking records. By the time he was sixteen, Louie was winning every race, setting new state records, and would soon become the fastest high school miler in American history.

At age nineteen, Louie became the youngest runner to make the US Olympic track team, competing in the 1936 games in Berlin, Germany. Though he ran well, he did not win his races.

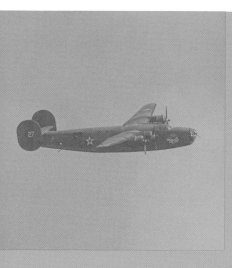

He was too young for the world stage. He then set his sights on the 1940 Olympics, but that was not to be. World War II* interrupted his life—along with millions of others—when he was drafted into the air corps* as a bombardier.

Louie's life moved from prankster to runner to soldier to survivor. He and his best friend were the only crew members alive after their B-24 crashed into the Pacific Ocean. For forty-seven days, in a feat of survival that could be called miraculous, these two men fought sharks, captured rainwater for drinking, fished for something to eat, and held on for dear life during fierce storms that threatened to kill them.

When they finally spotted land they were ecstatic, but joy quickly dissolved upon realizing it was a Japanese island. Now they were prisoners of war. Herded into crude huts, forced into hard labor, and beaten by the guards, life seemed unbearable. They survived the ocean for this? Though many men died from starvation, disease, or beatings in these POW (prisoner of war) camps, Louie survived. When the war finally ended, Louie returned to the United States.

Louie got married and tried to live a normal life, but he could not. He had nightmares about the horrors of the POW camp. He dreamed of returning to Japan to find and kill the men who had tortured him. The desire for revenge controlled him. Life became unbearable for his wife and new baby. His wife knew Louie needed help, so she begged him to go to a Billy Graham crusade with her. Though it took more than one sermon, Louie finally found true peace in Jesus.

Soon, Louie's obsession with returning to Japan to kill his tormentors changed into a mission to return and extend forgiveness to them. He had experienced the freedom forgiveness brings, and he wanted to offer that freedom to those who had abused him. Five years after the war ended Louie went back to Japan. He shook hands with each of his former captors and gave them the gift of forgiveness, that they too might be free. Louie's heart had been imprisoned behind bars of revenge; forgiveness was the key to his freedom.

---

* See Reference Points on page 33.

questions about forgiveness

- Discuss forgiveness as being the key to freedom.
- In what ways is the desire for revenge like being in prison?
- Why do you think Louie felt that he needed to meet with his former captors face-to-face?

practicing forgiveness

Louie felt that it was important to see his former captors face-to-face. That took a lot of courage and effort. Sometimes, if you need to forgive someone—or ask them to forgive you—it may seem easier to call, or send a text or e-mail. But if possible you should talk to them in person. This will help you build a stronger relationship with them and show them that you are sincere.

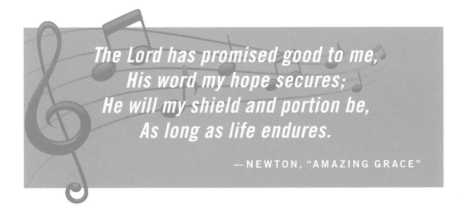

The Lord has promised good to me,
His word my hope secures;
He will my shield and portion be,
As long as life endures.

—NEWTON, "AMAZING GRACE"

praying together for forgiveness

Deliverer from evil, Rescuer from our natural ways, Savior of our souls, we give You thanks for the freedom that can be ours through forgiveness. As we extend the gift of forgiveness, You give the gift of peace. Help us follow You in forgiving, just as You forgave us. Amen.

As a family you might want to read about the POW experience of Louie Zamperini in the book, *Unbroken.*

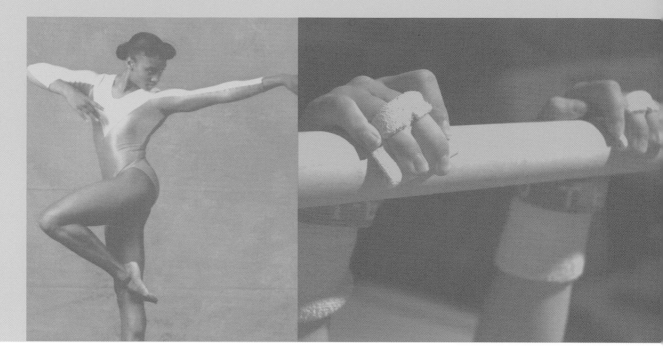

grace in motion

forgiveness is a gift of love

Gymnastics is a sport of elegant grace, intense focus, and physical endurance. Watching young gymnasts tumbling and catapulting through the air is like watching birds in flight. That's what Kim Anthony thought when she first saw the summer Olympics as an eight-year-old.

Kim was born in the poor section of Richmond, Virginia. Her parents had a rocky relationship, but they loved their baby. The army took them to Germany for two years where Kim's father and other black soldiers suffered racial abuse. To cope with the taunting, he and his friends began abusing drugs and alcohol. Even after returning home to the United States, he continued this lifestyle and, as always, when a parent makes unhealthy choices the whole family suffers.

In kindness, God provides touches of comfort and hope for those who cry out to Him. For Kim, that hope often came through her grandmother, Justine, who loved Jesus. While Kim's father drifted in and out of her life and her mother worked multiple jobs to provide for the family, Grandma Justine provided a measure of peace and stability to Kim's life.

For You, Lord, are good, and ready to forgive, /And abundant in lovingkindness to all who call upon You.
—PSALM 86:5

It was Jesus, Kim realized, not success in gymnastics, who could give her peace.

Then dawned the summer that changed Kim's life. Watching the Olympics on television, she was captured by the sport of gymnastics. The control, the freedom, and the power of the athletes spoke to her. She longed for what she saw, young women with total control. Lonely from her daddy's absence, Kim felt gymnastics would make him proud of her and maybe he would love her more.

Kim began practicing what she'd seen on television. By jumping off the steps of her house, learning to balance and twirl on top of a concrete block wall, and practicing cartwheels, flips, and aerials (a cartwheel using no hands), Kim taught herself gymnastics. She was fearless.

One Saturday morning two years later, Kim and her mom rode the city bus to a training gym where Kim could finally receive real lessons. The coaches were astounded at what this child had taught herself, all without the safety of mats and spotters (people who help gymnasts avoid injury while practicing). Kim was delighted when the coaches offered her an invitation to join a competitive gymnastics team.

Kim started intense training, and her mother took on an even heavier workload in order to pay for the lessons and competitions. In her heart Kim hoped to win her daddy back to their family. Sometimes when he came home, Kim felt nervous, but she also eagerly wanted him to stay. Then, after a few days he'd abruptly disappear, leaving her feeling abandoned and confused again. And her hardworking, patient mother never said a negative word about him.

Kim achieved success. She won state, regional, and international meets, and eventually—at age sixteen—competed for a place on the US Olympic team. When the time came for choosing a college, she was offered a scholarship to join the UCLA (University of California at Los Angeles) women's gymnastics team. While attending UCLA, a friend talked to her about a relationship with Jesus Christ. It was Jesus, Kim realized, not success in gymnastics, who could give her peace. She gratefully welcomed Jesus into her heart.

College brought more medals as Kim became the first African-American UCLA gymnast to become a four-time national champion. She traveled around the world with Athletes in Action* competing and speaking. But the most important competition for Kim during those years was the one for her heart. Who would control her heart and life? Whose will would she follow? Kim was learning that she must ultimately please Christ, and He wanted her to love her father and forgive him, even though he had hurt her greatly.

In 2009, Kim, now married and the mother of two boys, traveled back to Virginia to meet with her father. She told him how she felt as a little girl and how badly she missed his presence. Through tears she spoke of her love for him, and then said she forgave him for his poor choices. Because of Jesus her new purpose in life included following His teachings in the Bible. Kim understood that forgiveness was a choice. Forgiving was a gift of love that changed Kim and gave her a new relationship with her father.

* See Reference Points on page 33.

questions about forgiveness

- Fathers and mothers are imperfect people; they make mistakes that sometimes hurt their children. Forgiveness is healing medicine for all families.
- What can we learn from Kim's story about the power of forgiveness in her life and in her father's life?
- Have you ever been angry at your mother or father for a mistake they made? What is the best way to talk to your parents about that hurt?

practicing forgiveness

It hurts to fight with your friends and siblings, but it is especially painful when you have a conflict with your parents. If this is your situation, you need to talk to your mom or dad. First, pray that God will give you courage and that He will help you to be respectful in your words and attitude. Then, when you're ready and when you can talk with them alone, tell your parents what's troubling you.

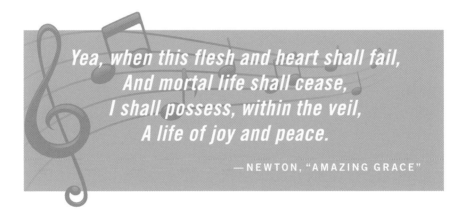

Yea, when this flesh and heart shall fail,
And mortal life shall cease,
I shall possess, within the veil,
A life of joy and peace.

—NEWTON, "AMAZING GRACE"

praying together for forgiveness

Perfect Father, help us who are parents to confess our mistakes to our children. Help us teach and model forgiveness as a family. Help each of us, parent and child, put our hand in Your hand so that You might be our guide in life. When we walk closely with You, we will learn to forgive freely, graciously, and generously. And when we do, You will smile. Amen.

a nation torn apart

forgiveness is a door of hope

Forgiveness means giving up the right to get even or to punish another person who has offended you. Choosing to forgive is a miracle of grace. But there are some offenses that seem impossible to forgive. This is the story of a country of millions of people that is showing the world the hope of forgiveness that only Jesus Christ can bring.

The small African country of Rwanda underwent a brutal genocide* in 1994. The details behind the story are quite complicated; the short version is that certain people stirred up hatred of one race of people (the Hutu) against another (the Tutsi), resulting in the deaths of 1,117,000 innocents in three months.

It is very hard to understand how this happened. We wonder why God didn't stop these people who roamed the streets and villages of Rwanda killing every Tutsi they could find. We wonder how such evil gains control. We wonder how to stop killing on this earth. And the answer is found only in Jesus and in forgiveness.

Help us, O God of our salvation, for the glory of Your name; /And deliver us and forgive our sins for Your name's sake.
—PSALM 79:9

There are some offenses that seem impossible to forgive.

Immaculée was a young Tutsi girl who survived the killing of her people and her family. She and her brothers ran away from the bands of young men who hunted them and other Tutsis with knives, machetes, and spears. After escaping to a pastor friend's house where they were hidden, the young men, including her brother, were forced to leave in the middle of the night a few days later. But Immaculée and six other women were hidden in a small bathroom that even the pastor's children did not know existed in his house. If the pastor and his family, who were Hutu, were discovered protecting Tutsis, they too would have been killed.

Unable to make a sound for fear of being discovered and terrified for their lives, these women remained in the tiny bathroom for three months. They could not lie down. They never went outside. They had very little food, because the pastor did not let his wife or children know the

---

* See Reference Points on page 33.

women were hiding for fear they would tell; he could only bring them a few leftovers when no one was watching.

Immaculée wrote in her book, *Left to Tell*, about praying constantly for God to give her peace and protection. She wrote, "Even a few minutes not spent in prayer . . . became an invitation for Satan to stab me with . . . doubt and self-pity."[1] She also wrote about the anger she felt. One day the pastor came to tell the women how bad the situation had become. He told them how Tutsis had fled to churches to hide, thinking they would be safe there, but that the angry mobs burned down the churches while the people were still inside. He told the women that all schools and businesses and markets were closed until the killing was over.

"At that moment," Immaculée wrote, "I was angrier than I'd ever been before—more than I believed was even possible. I was angry at the pastor for telling us such horrific details. . . . I was angry at the government. . . . I was angry at rich countries for not stopping the slaughter. . . . I'd never done anything violent before, but at that moment I wished I had a gun."[2] She knew she should forgive the killers, but she felt they did not deserve to be forgiven.

A week or more passed with Immaculée praying over and over, "Show me how to forgive, Lord." Then, one night after listening to a dying baby cry outside the bathroom window, God spoke to her heart, *"The baby is with Me. . . . Forgive them; for they know not what they do."*[3] Jesus said that on the cross when He was unjustly killed. And because He forgave, Immaculée knew—and so can you and I—that He could give her the strength to forgive.

As the Anglican bishop* of Rwanda, John Rucyahana experienced the horror of what happened in 1994. Today, as a pastor, he is helping lead his nation back to God, teaching that God did not abandon Rwanda to the evil, but instead He was there comforting the dying and saving many by miracles. "Sometimes evil has its day, because men have so turned themselves over to it. But even then, God does not abandon them. God waits to perform a miracle." Bishop John tells all who will listen, "Without God, I would hate such killers with all my heart. But with God I can truly say that I love them."[4]

Forgiving is impossible on our own. Children and adults alike need the life-changing power of God to truly forgive. God can heal broken hearts and minds and lives. If God can work this miracle of forgiveness in Rwanda, He can help you forgive, too.

---

* See Reference Points on page 33.

questions about forgiveness

- What do you think takes more courage, forgiving or taking revenge? Why do you think so?
- Do you have someone that you need to forgive? If you're not ready to forgive them, what can you do to prepare your heart?
- Are you willing to let God change you as He did Immaculee? Will you believe that "nothing will be impossible with God" (Luke 1:37)?

practicing forgiveness

Forgiveness is impossible without God working in our hearts. Immaculee wanted to kill those who were killing her people, and she knew that was wrong, so she prayed and prayed. And that is the key to any forgiveness—asking God to change our hearts.

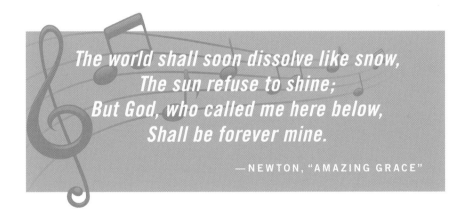

The world shall soon dissolve like snow,
The sun refuse to shine;
But God, who called me here below,
Shall be forever mine.

—NEWTON, "AMAZING GRACE"

praying together for forgiveness

O God of mercy, God of miracles, would You perform a miracle in my heart? Would You grant me faith to believe You for the impossible? Would You make our family willing forgivers? Give us each a vision for what You can do and the hope that is ours when we become like Jesus and forgive. May it be so. Amen.

the voice of peace

forgiveness is a gift of peace

Many of us face the question of forgiveness with family members, classmates, or neighbors, but few will ever be faced with the decision to forgive a killer.

The Bible tells us that God is just. Scriptures like Romans 2:11, which says, "There is no partiality with God," mean that He doesn't favor one person or one race of people over another. All are created by God in His image. But because we are imperfect people, we live with injustice. Joseph was favored over his brothers and that led to decades of problems in his family. In Rwanda, the Hutus were taught and encouraged to hate the Tutsis, which in time led to the murder of millions of people. You, too, will face injustice in your life that will leave you with a choice to forgive or to seek revenge.

In the 1950s and '60s, injustice abounded in the United States as white people tried to keep black people from attaining equality in work and education and even in everyday things like riding the same bus, using the same bathrooms, or drinking from the same water fountains. At

> Let the peace of Christ rule in your hearts.
> —COLOSSIANS 3:13

> *Love is the only force capable of transforming an enemy into a friend.*

a rally in Marion, Alabama, a young black man was shot by policemen while protecting his mother from being beaten by a state trooper. In Little Rock, Arkansas, when the government was attempting to integrate the public schools, black children had to be escorted by US Marshals* so they could enter the buildings safely. In other places, the homes and churches of black families were often burned to frighten their owners.

In the midst of these years of injustice, a brave voice called for forgiveness and love to rule over hatred and revenge. That was the voice of Reverend Martin Luther King Jr. who said, "Love even for our enemies is the key to the solution of the problems of our world. . . . Returning hate for hate multiplies hate. Darkness cannot drive out darkness; only light can do that. Hate cannot drive out hate; only love can do that. . . . Love is the only force capable of transforming an enemy

---

* See Reference Points on page 33.

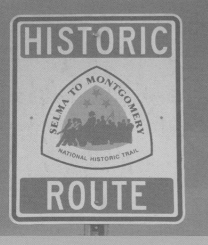

into a friend. . . . Hate destroys and tears down, . . . love creates and builds up."[1]

Reverend King was a leader for great good, because he encouraged all African-Americans to forgive and love even though they were being treated unjustly. In Marion, Alabama, during the memorial service for young Jimmie Jackson who was shot protecting his mother, not one of the thousands of people who attended his service spoke of revenge. Instead, all who listened heard words of faith and encouragement to love and forgive. Reverend King challenged the people to pray for the police and to forgive the ones who were persecuting. Remarkably, Jimmie's parents refused to give in to hate. They knew being angry could not bring their son back.

Even young children understood the message to forgive. Little six-year-old Ruby Bridges was escorted to school by US Marshals in New Orleans. She was yelled at by angry whites, but instead of yelling back she prayed as she walked. "They need praying for,"[2] she said when her teacher asked her what she was saying as she walked. Ruby had heard in church the story of Jesus saying, "Father, forgive them for they know not what they are doing" (see Luke 23:34), and she believed it was true for her, too.

Reverend King said, "It is impossible to love one's enemies without first forgiving those who inflict evil and injury on us. Forgiveness does not mean ignoring what has been done. It is a fresh start and a new beginning."[3]

Forgiveness is necessary for every person of every age for all of life. There will always be injustice in families, because parents are not perfect and children want to be the favorite. There will be injustice in schools, because teachers sometimes favor certain students over others. And friends turn on friends saying things that aren't true. Every person alive has felt the desire to be better than someone else. And when that sinful desire hurts another person with words or actions, it is time to seek forgiveness.

Forgiveness is like crossing a stream by moving from one rock to the next. Begin by stepping on the first stone. Ask God to help you want to forgive. Then, when the time is right, take the next step of giving forgiveness.

questions about forgiveness

- What did Reverend King mean when he said, "It is impossible to love one's enemies without first forgiving"?
- How do we learn to forgive?
- How do we forgive while not ignoring the damage or the pain?

practicing forgiveness

Forgiveness should be part of your life for as long as you live. There will always be injustices in our world. People will get hurt, be angry, and will sometimes do extreme things to try to get even with their oppressors. But you can be a voice of calm, peace, and forgiveness. Choose to be a peacemaker rather than a troublemaker.

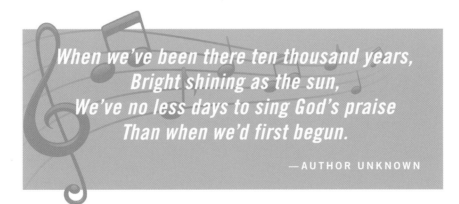

When we've been there ten thousand years,
Bright shining as the sun,
We've no less days to sing God's praise
Than when we'd first begun.

—AUTHOR UNKNOWN

praying together for forgiveness

Father, because Jesus forgave His killers even before they had finished their evil work, we too can forgive. Injustices, offenses, and rejections can all be overcome by the work of forgiveness made possible by the cross. May our obedient forgiveness open doors of peace, love, and reconciliation—that the world may know Jesus is Lord—for His sake because He showed us the way. Amen.

FORGIVENESS IN ACTION

In a short story titled *The Capitol of the World*, Nobel prize-winning author Ernest Hemmingway tells about a father and a teenage son, Paco, whose relationship breaks down. After the son runs away from home, the father begins a long journey in search of him. Finally, as a last resort, the man puts an ad in the local newspaper in Madrid. It reads, "Dear Paco, Meet me in front of the newspaper office tomorrow at noon . . . all is forgiven . . . I love you." The next morning in front of the newspaper office were eight hundred men named Paco, desiring to restore a broken relationship.[1]

Forgiveness is inspiring. What stories have you read or heard about people who were once hurt or angry with each other but were later restored through the grace of forgiveness? Record summaries of these stories here, and keep this as a reminder of the power and Christ-likeness of forgiveness.

date

REFERENCE POINTS

DAY TWO: A **famine** is a widespread, extreme shortage of food that can be caused by a lack of rainfall or diseased crops.

DAY THREE: **New Zealand** is a country in the southwestern Pacific Ocean consisting of two main parts—the North Island and the South Island—and many smaller islands.
Utu is a tradition among some tribal cultures in the South Pacific. It is the practice of revenge—retaliating for every injury or insult.

DAY FOUR: **World War II** was the war from 1939 to 1945 between the Allies (Great Britain, France, the Soviet Union, the United States, and others) and the Axis (Germany, Italy, Japan, and others).

The **air corps** was officially known as the United States Army Air Corps during World War II. Later it became part of the United States Air Force.

DAY FIVE: **Athletes in Action** is a global sports ministry with the goal of having a Christ follower on every team, in every sport, and in every nation.

DAY SIX: **Genocide** is intentional killing with the plan to destroy a whole national or ethnic group.

An **Anglican bishop** is a leader of high rank in the Anglican Church.

DAY SEVEN: **US Marshals** are law officials serving through the Federal Court system. Their job includes protecting people while carrying out a court ruling.

notes

Pages viii-ix

1. Henri Nouwen in Johann Arnold, *Why Forgive?* (Farmington, PA: Plough Publishing House, 2000), 100.

2. C. S. Lewis, *The Four Loves* (Orlando: Harcourt Brace & Company, 1988), 121.

Day 1

1. John Newton, *The Life and Spirituality of John Newton* (Vancouver, Canada: Regent College Publishing, 1998), 31.

2. Steve Turner, *Amazing Grace: The Story of America's Most Beloved Song* (New York: HarperCollins, 2002), 65.

3. John Newton and Richard Cecil, *The Works of the Reverend J. Newton with the Memoirs of the Author and General Remarks on His Life, Connections, and Character* (1824; http://books.google.com, 2006), 97.

Day 6

1. Immaculée Ilibagiza with Steve Erwin, *Left to Tell: Discovering God Amidst the Rwandan Holocaust* (Carlsbad, CA: Hay House, 2006), 85.

2. Ibid., 88.

3. Ibid., 94.

4. John Rucyahana, *The Bishop of Rwanda* (Nashville: Thomas Nelson, 2006) xvi.

Day 7

1. Martin Luther King, Jr., *Strength to Love* (Minneapolis: Fortress Press, 1977), 49–50, 53–54.

2. Ruby Bridges in Johann Arnold, *Why Forgive?* (Farmington, PA: Plough Publishing House, 2000), 34.

3. King, 50.

Page 30

1. John Maxwell, *21 Indispensable Qualities of a Leader* (Nashville: Thomas Nelson, 1990), 110.

photo credits

FRONT COVER

Louis Zamperini—© Bettmann/Corbis
Shepherd and flock—©Bigstock.com
(nopow)
Engraving of ship loaded with
slaves 1881—iStockphoto.com
(Grafissimo)
Kim Anthony—Courtesy of
Kim Anthony

BACK COVER

Bishop John Rucyahana—Courtesy
of the Stone Ward Agency
B-24 bomber—©Oldedawg |
Dreamstime.com
Hands on bar—©iStockphoto.com
(nazarethman)
Historical route sign—Carol M.
Highsmith, Library of Congress

PAGE VI

Boy holding dandelion—
©iStockphoto.com (Nick
Thompson, Igor Stepovik)

PAGE 2 JOHN NEWTON

John Newton's epitaph—
©iStockphoto.com (PeskyMonkey)
Engraving of ship loaded with slaves
1881—©iStockphoto.com
(Grafissimo)
"Amazing Grace" Calligraphy—Used
by permission of Galen Berry,
MarbleArt.us
Boy playing in puddle—©Omenn |
Dreamstime.com

PAGE 4

Shackles—©Bigstock.com
(Martin Stubbs)

PAGE 6 JOSEPH

Joseph's Dream—GoodSalt Images
(Standard Publishing)
Shepherd and flock—©Bigstock.com
(nopow)
Caravan—©Bigstock.com
(theworldeffect)
Joseph's Brothers Ask for Grain—
GoodSalt Images (Standard
Publishing)

PAGE 8

Joseph Makes Himself Known to
his Brothers—GoodSalt Images
(Lars Justinen)

PAGE 10 TARORE

Map—©iStockphoto.com (KeithBinns)
New Zealand—©Bigstock.com
(Ruthie44)
Interior of the Rangiatea Church at Otaki.
Denton, Frank J, 1869-1963: Collection
of negatives, prints and albums. Ref:
PA1-o-131-28. Alexander Turnbull
Library, Wellington, New Zealand.
http://beta.natlib.govt.nz/
records/22342707
Photograph of Te Rongopai a Ruka
(The Gospel of Luke in Maori)
by Bruce Hutton QSM, FPSNZ.
© Bible Society New Zealand.
Used with permission.

PAGE 12

Straw bag—©iStockphoto.com
(tweetyclaw)

PAGE 14 LOUIS ZAMPERINI

Bell tower—©iStockphoto.com
(Hohenhaus)
POW Camp Hanawa01—Still
picture records at the National
Archives courtesy of http://home.
comcast.net/~japanpow/Recovery/
Recovery.htm
Louis Zamperini with his brother—
© Bettmann/Corbis
Louis Zamperini—© Bettmann/Corbis

PAGE 16

B-24 bomber—©Oldedawg |
Dreamstime.com

PAGE 18 KIM ANTHONY

Kim Anthony—Courtesy of
Kim Anthony
Hands on bar—©iStockphoto.com
(nazarethman)
Kim with her grandma—Courtesy
of Kim Anthony
Kim with her mom—Courtesy
of Kim Anthony

PAGE 20

Gold medals—©123rf.com
(Ivonne Wierink)

PAGE 22 RWANDA

Bishop John Rucyahana—Courtesy
of the Stone Ward Agency
Map—©Olira |Dreamstime
Hands—©iStockphoto.com
(JasonRWarren)
Bathroom—©iStockphoto.com
(shaunl)

PAGE 24

Praying girl—©iStockphoto.com
(ozgurdonmaz)

PAGE 26 MARTIN LUTHER KING, JR.

Martin Luther King, Jr.—Dick
DeMarsico, Library of Congress
King birth home—Library of Congress
School children—Thomas O'Halloran,
photographer, Library of Congress
Dexter Avenue Church—The George F.
Landegger collection of Alabama
photographs in Carol M. Highsmith's
America, Library of Congress

PAGE 28

Historical route sign—Carol M.
Highsmith, photographer, Library
of Congress

A LETTER FROM THE AUTHOR

Dear Reader,

My husband and I had six children in ten years. The wide range of their ages and personalities made leading our children in any kind of home-centered spiritual direction a daunting task. So when a parent asks me how to encourage a fifteen-year-old in his faith while not ignoring the childlike questions of his five-year-old sister, I understand the predicament.

Where can a parent find stories and learning activities that are relevant to all ages? That was my dilemma; I could find no resources for a family like mine. I found lots of stories and songs for preschoolers and devotionals for teens, but nothing that would appeal to all of my children *together*.

What I did discover was that the best and easiest vehicle for transferring truth to my children was through stories. Whatever success we might have achieved in spiritually training our family came through shared stories of faith and discussions with our kids about taking God's truth with them into their lives. From that experience was born my dream to create resources to help moms and dads who want to be instrumental in raising children who are Christ followers.

Parents need something that works, something that is easy, something that requires no preparation. These seven stories make that possible. And unlike most devotional books that feature different themes with each day's reading, this resource focuses on one character quality that all parents want to develop in their children—forgiveness. By reinforcing this one topic, my hope is that you and your family will grow in your understanding of both giving and receiving forgiveness and the freedom true forgiveness brings.

Thanks for using this short family devotional. I pray that you and your children will grow together as you're inspired by the great faith of these men and women whose stories I've shared.

Barbara Rainey

ABOUT THE AUTHOR

Barbara Rainey is the mother of six adult children and the "Mimi" of eighteen grandchildren. She and her husband, Dennis, give leadership to FamilyLife, a ministry committed to helping marriages and families survive and thrive in our generation. Barbara has written several books, including *Thanksgiving: A Time to Remember, Barbara and Susan's Guide to the Empty Nest,* and *When Christmas Came.* The Raineys live in Little Rock, Arkansas.

You can read more from Barbara online at FamilyLifeMomblog.com.